Keeper of the Freedom

Companion Journal to Friends and Gems Freedom,
and A One Year Bride
By
Bonnie McPhail

Unless otherwise indicated, all scripture quotes are taken from *The Message and the New King James Version of the Bible*

15 14 13 12 11 10 09 08   8 7 6 5 4 3 2 1

Keeper of the Freedom
 Companion Journal to Friends and Gems Freedom
And *A One Year Bride*

ISBN-13: 978-1463581916 ISBN-10:1463581912

Visit www.thefathersmarket.com to view the author's web page and order handcrafted gifts and books.

Printed in the United States of America.

Dear Friends,

In the day and age in which we live, with our busy and hectic lives it is difficult to find time to read God's word and let it speak personally to us.

We lay aside the deepest dreams and longings of our heart for the clutter and demands of our lives.

Journaling is a powerful way for the Lord to speak to you. He wants to! He wants to tell you specific nuggets of truth, those "gems" that will help and encourage you. He wants to explain situations and the solutions you need. He wants to bless and grace you with his presence. He wants to be your friend.

Keeper of the Freedom contains the first chapter from *A One Year Bride* the companion book to *Friends and Gems Freedom*. This is a series of three books. You can use them together or separately; or give them to a special friend who needs to find freedom and soar to new dreams.

The Lord is the keeper of your freedom and he cares about everything that concerns you!
Many Blessings to you!

Bonnie McPhail

✿ Dedicated to ♥

My Mother Jeanne Craigue who has always believed in
my dreams and continues to encourage them.
My sisters Ann Formichella, and Tina Chute both
examples of overcoming adversity,
strength and character.
The three of you have been my inspiration.
I love you!

Author

Bonnie McPhail is an artist and published author, with well over forty books in print including fiction, bible studies and craft workshops, devotionals and journals.

She is active in women's ministry. She also has an associate degree in nursing from the University of New York, and is a graduate of Rhema Bible Training Center

Bonnie's nursing background gives her insights into women's physical—as well as spiritual and emotional—needs. She has a true heart for people who are hurting and wounded. Bonnie is a speaker and teacher, and is available for women's conferences and workshops.

Bonnie is also a licensed Assembly of God Minister and she is a Pastor to the women she ministers to.

View her work at: www.thefathersmarket.com

Or contact her to schedule an event at your church at:
angelcare6@yahoo.com

Excerpt from

A One Year Bride

By

Bonnie McPhail

"It is God who arms me with strength
and makes my way perfect."
Psalm 18:32 N.I.V.

Megan awakens in a hospital bed, memories of blood, screams, screeching metal and the smell of gasoline assault her being.

Images of broken, unrecognizable bodies and a man sitting on the side of the road with his head in his hands flash through her mind. He walks away while her beloved family is dead.

A monstrous anger rises up like bile in the back of her throat and she shakes with the force of it.

A hand lies on her shoulder; a deeply masculine yet familiar voice is filled with calm gentleness and tinged with sorrow. "I can't imagine what you are going through; just know I am here for you if you need me."

Recognition comes and she realizes it is James, her husband Eric's best friend and child hood buddy.

His ebony eyes are pools of sadness, the depths of his own loss glittering with unshed tears. His handsomely chiseled face is so familiar. There was a time when she almost chose him instead of Eric. Now his presence is so very welcome she has no one left. They are all gone.

"James what am I going to do?" Embarrassed at the sudden rush of tears she turns to the wall, drawing into a fetal position. Raw pain rips open uncontrollable sobs, she has no choice but to release them, choking and gulping for air; she realizes the screams she hears are her own.

Chapter One

A single candle illuminated the darkness; eerie shadows danced across the wall. The electricity had been turned off days ago, a half eaten can of tuna and a cup of warm tap water; evidence of not being able to cook.

Megan's eyes were puffy and swollen, tear stained mascara ran down both sides of her face and black spots dropped across bills scattered on the table.

A loud knock sounded at the door quickly wiping her tears and blowing her nose Megan pushed her sweat soaked hair off her face and adjusted the two day old wrinkled clothing she wore. "Just a minute I'll be right there."

Opening the door she was surprised to see James standing there. Even after all these years his handsomely chiseled features, ebony eyes and dazzling smile still took her breath away.

Right now his wavy black hair was tucked under his baseball cap turned around backwards and there was a weekends worth of scratchy beard on his unshaved face. It only added to the instant attraction she felt. She quickly shoved it into the recesses of her mind. There was no way she was going to go there.

Freshly grilled burgers and fries caught her attention and her stomach cramped with hunger. She was embarrassed at the growling noises that gave it away.

James heart lurched when he saw the conditions she was living in. A wave of protectiveness lit his insides. He so longed to take it away, shield her and make it better.

Their fingertips brushed as he handed her the food. Electric warmth spread down his arm and his body responded in a way he didn't want it to.

Guilt roared through his being, this was his best friend's wife; his dead best friend. He should not be feeling what he was feeling.

"Thought you might like something hot."

"Thanks so much I really appreciate your thoughtfulness."

"No problem just happened to be in the neighborhood."

She avoided his gaze looking instead at the food in his hand.

Sadness overwhelmed him at what he saw. It wasn't so much the ruined makeup it was the haunted, empty look in her eyes.

Megan was tall and strikingly beautiful; chestnut hair styled in the latest bob, slender and athletic, she was every guys dream. Her most amazing feature was her unusual emerald green eyes. You could lose yourself in those hypnotic eyes and he had on more than one occasion.

More than her looks was what shown from the inside. She had no clue that she was beautiful and didn't care. She loved from the depths of her being and reached out to anyone in need. Her warmth and contagious smile could light up a room.

Now all he saw on her beautiful features was hopelessness and fear. It ripped his heart out. What he wanted to do was take her in his arms; shield her from the hurt.

"Want to share?" she asked.

"Nah, I brought enough for two, well actually for three." There was a hint of a knowing smile behind his words.

At the mention of three she inadvertently placed her hand on her growing abdomen; a loving, gentle gesture for the life growing inside her.

"Have you been to the doctor lately?"

"He says she's perfect."

"So it's a girl?"

"Yeah I just found out yesterday." Her voice sounded hollow.

"How many weeks along are you?"

"Twenty, she'll be here in four months; just in time for Christmas." The brave tiny smile and the tears glittering behind her lashes broke his heart.

"Come on let's sit over on the couch there is more room." She said.

She led the way and he sat beside her. Not even realizing the effect her close proximity was having on him she made it worse by leaning with her back against his chest. "I'm so grateful for your friendship James I don't know what I would have done these past few months without you."

Megan relished in the warmth and strength of his muscled body. She felt a twinge of guilt at sitting so close to him but she pushed it aside for her own need of human contact. She had always considered James her brother anyhow, and that wasn't about to change. Times like this she missed Eric so much. His loss was tangible and the air was thick with it.

No one would understand that better than James. He and Eric had been inseparable since they were boys growing up in the same neighborhood. James always took the punches for Eric until he got bigger and could fend for himself.

The flickering candle brought back memories of the three of them sitting around the campfire at youth retreat.

"Do you remember that time when you me and Eric went camping together?"

"Yeah you mean the time you and Eric both ganged up on me and tried to convert me?"

"Well, we did double team you didn't we?" she said with a laugh.

In his mind's eye he was back at the campsite; a spring retreat trip to *Yosemite National Park*. The entire youth group had worked tirelessly all summer to raise the money so everyone could go. Eric and Megan newly dating had invited James along.

The three of them were sitting around the campfire comfortable sounds of guitar music, and laughter blended into the night.

The boy's campsite was separate and carefully monitored for pranks and the ravages of young men's hormones, but for now supervised co-ed free time was being allowed.

Visions of the striking couple with him played in his mind. Eric strikingly handsome; tall tanned and muscular with California blonde blue eyed good looks and she nearby nearly as tall as he her auburn hair hanging in shimmering beauty to her waist.

They were deeply in love with each other and the God he wanted nothing to do with; the God who let his father throw his mother down the stairs in a drunken rage; and who beat him senseless with the belt when he tried to help her. No, he would not serve that God no matter what they said.

His lack of faith and belief was the very reason Megan had chosen Eric over him, both had been vying for her attention for months. If he hadn't loved Eric like his own brother there would have been a fight over it.

Sitting beside her on the couch now nearly ten years later he was struck with the fact that time had only made her even more appealing. At twenty eight years of age she had matured into a stunningly beautiful woman.

She never had a clue that he loved her then and yes he had to admit to himself, loved her still.

"James are you okay?" The soft mellowness of her voice broke into his reverie and brought him back to the present.

"Yeah I'm okay but more importantly are you okay?"

"Well, I'm doing as well as can be expected. The doctor says the baby is fine that's what matters most to me."

What she really wanted to say was that she had no food left, the small inheritance from her parent's estate had run out a week ago, the house was in the third month of foreclosure, and yesterday her car was repossessed. Her faith was running on gas fumes.

"I'll be okay the Lord always provides." She said more to herself than to him.

Her words grated and made him uneasy. How could she continue to serve a God who allowed her parents who were both Pastors and the best people he ever knew die. How could a loving God take her husband when after ten years of trying they finally conceived a new life?

He felt disgusted as he sat in the dark room beside her. It didn't take a genius to see the dire straits she was in. After all the years of knowing her he could read between the lines of what she wasn't saying.

Maybe she thought her God would take care of her, but if he had anything to do with it the idea he had would be what took care of her not her God.

He would have to move quickly, she was running out of time.

_____

_____

_____

_____

_____

_____

_____

_____

_____

_____

_____

_____

_____

_____

_____

_____

_____

_____

"God charts the road you take."
Psalm 1:4 T.M.

_____

_____

_____

_____

_____

_____

_____

_____

_____

_____

_____

_____

_____

_____

_____

_____

_____

_____

_____

_____

_____

_____

"Real help comes from God.
Your blessing clothes your people." Psalm 3:8 T.M

_____
_____
_____
_____
_____
_____
_____
_____
_____
_____
_____
_____
_____
_____
_____
_____
_____
_____
_____
_____
_____
_____
_____

"When I call, give me answers. God, take my side!
Psalm 4:1 T.M

"But you'll welcome us with open arms when we run for cover to you."
Psalm 5:11 T.M

"You are famous God, for welcoming God - seekers, for decking us out in delight." Psalm 5:12 T.M

_____
_____
_____
_____
_____
_____
_____
_____
_____
_____
_____
_____
_____
_____
_____
_____
_____
_____
_____
_____
_____
_____
_____

"Do you think you can mess with the dreams of the poor? You can't, for God makes their dreams come true." Psalm 14:6 T.M.

"I call to you God, because I am sure of an answer."
Psalm 17:6 T.M.

_____
_____
_____
_____
_____
_____
_____
_____
_____
_____
_____
_____
_____
_____
_____
_____
_____
_____
_____
_____
_____

"God made my life complete when I placed all the pieces before him."
Psalm 18:20 T.M.

"God rewrote the text of my life when I opened the book
of my heart to his eyes." Psalm 18:24 T.M.

"What a God! His road stretches straight and smooth!"
Psalm 18:30a T.M.

_____

_____

_____

_____

_____

_____

_____

_____

_____

_____

_____

_____

_____

_____

_____

_____

_____

_____

_____

_____

_____

_____

_____

"Every God-direction is road tested. Everyone who runs toward him
makes it." Psalm 18:30b

_____

_____

_____

_____

_____

_____

_____

_____

_____

_____

_____

_____

_____

_____

_____

_____

_____

_____

_____

_____

_____

_____

"Is not this the God who armed me, then aimed me in the right direction?"
Psalm 18:31 T.M.

_____

_____

_____

_____

_____

_____

_____

_____

_____

_____

_____

_____

_____

_____

_____

_____

_____

_____

_____

_____

_____

_____

"You protect me with salvation-armor; you hold me up with a firm hand, caress me with your gentle ways." Psalm 18:32 T.M.

_____

_____

_____

_____

_____

_____

_____

_____

_____

_____

_____

_____

_____

_____

_____

_____

_____

_____

_____

_____

_____

_____

"You cleared the ground under me so my footing was firm."
Psalm 18:34 T.M.

"The revelation of God is whole and pulls our lives together."
Psalm 19:7 T.M.

_____

_____

_____

_____

_____

_____

_____

_____

_____

_____

_____

_____

_____

_____

_____

_____

_____

_____

_____

_____

_____

_____

_____

_____

"The signposts of God are clear and point out the right road."
Psalm 19:8 T. M.

_____
_____
_____
_____
_____
_____
_____
_____
_____
_____
_____
_____
_____
_____
_____
_____
_____
_____
_____
_____
_____
_____

"The life-maps of God are right showing me the way to joy."
Psalm 19: 9 T.M.

"God's word warns us of danger and directs us to hidden danger."
Psalm 19:11 T.M.

"That clinches it__help's coming, and answer's on the way, everything's going to work out." Psalm 20:6 T.M.

"He has never wandered off to do his own thing;
he has been right there, listening." Psalm 22:24 T.M.

"Down-and-outers sit at God's table and eat their fill."
Psalm 22:26 T. M.

_____

_____

_____

_____

_____

_____

_____

_____

_____

_____

_____

_____

_____

_____

_____

_____

_____

_____

_____

_____

_____

_____

*"True to your word, you let me catch my breath
and send me in the right direction." Psalm 23:3 T.M.*

"Even when the way goes through Death valley,
I'm not afraid when you walk at my side." Psalm 23:4 T.M.

"Your trusty shepherd's crook makes me feel secure."
Psalm 23:4 T.M.

"You serve me a six-course dinner right in front of my enemies.
Psalm 23:5 T. M.

"You revive my drooping head; my cup brims with blessing."
Psalm 23:5 T. M.

"Your beauty and love chase after me every day of my life."
Psalm 23:6 T. M.

_____

_____

_____

_____

_____

_____

_____

_____

_____

_____

_____

_____

_____

_____

_____

_____

_____

_____

_____

_____

_____

_____

_____

_____

"I'm back home in the house of God for the rest of my life."
Psalm 23:6 T. M.

_____

_____

_____

_____

_____

_____

_____

_____

_____

_____

_____

_____

_____

_____

_____

_____

_____

_____

_____

_____

_____

_____

"God is at their side; with God's help they can make it."
Psalm 24:5 T.M.

_____

_____

_____

_____

_____

_____

_____

_____

_____

_____

_____

_____

_____

_____

_____

_____

_____

_____

_____

_____

_____

*"God is fair and just; He corrects the misdirected,
sends them in the right direction." Psalm 25:8 T.M.*

_____
_____
_____
_____
_____
_____
_____
_____
_____
_____
_____
_____
_____
_____
_____
_____
_____
_____
_____
_____
_____

"From now on every road you travel will take you to God."
Psalm 25:10 T. M.

"Follow the Covenant signs read the charted directions."
Psalm 25:10 T. M.

_____

_____

_____

_____

_____

_____

_____

_____

_____

_____

_____

_____

_____

_____

_____

_____

_____

_____

_____

_____

_____

_____

"God-friendship is for God-worshipers; they are the ones he confides in."
Psalm 25:14 T. M.

"If I keep my eyes on God, I won't trip over my own feet."
Psalm 25:15 T.M.

_____

_____

_____

_____

_____

_____

_____

_____

_____

_____

_____

_____

_____

_____

_____

_____

_____

_____

_____

_____

_____

_____

"Use all your skill to put me together; I wait so see your finished product."
Psalm 25:21 T.M.

"God, I love living with you, your house glows with your glory."
Psalm 26:8 T.M.

_____

_____

_____

_____

_____

_____

_____

_____

_____

_____

_____

_____

_____

_____

_____

_____

_____

_____

_____

_____

_____

_____

_____

"God holds me head and shoulders above all who try to pull me down."
Psalm 27:6 T.M.

"Point me down your highway, God; direct me along a well-lighted street."
Psalm 27:17 T.M.

"I'm sure now I'll see God's goodness in the exuberant earth. Stay with God! Take heart. Don't quit." Psalm 27:13 T.M.

_____

_____

_____

_____

_____

_____

_____

_____

_____

_____

_____

_____

_____

_____

_____

_____

_____

_____

_____

_____

_____

_____

"God is all strength for his people, ample refuge for his chosen leader; save your people and bless your heritage." Psalm 28:8 T.M.

_____

_____

_____

_____

_____

_____

_____

_____

_____

_____

_____

_____

_____

_____

_____

_____

_____

_____

_____

_____

_____

_____

_____

_____

"God makes his people strong. God gives his people peace."
Psalm 29.11 T.M.

"God, my God, I yelled for help and you put me together."
Psalm 30:2 T.M.

"The nights of crying your eyes out give way to days of laughter."
Psalm 30:5 T.M.

"God, my God, I can't thank you enough."
Psalm 30:12 T.M.

_____

_____

_____

_____

_____

_____

_____

_____

_____

_____

_____

_____

_____

_____

_____

_____

_____

_____

_____

_____

_____

_____

_____

"I've put my life in your hands. You won't drop me; you'll never let me down." Psalm 31:5 T.M.

"What a stack of blessing you have piled up for those who worship you."
Psalm 31:19 T.M.

"Ready and waiting for all who run to you to escape an unkind world. You hide them safely away from opposition." Psalm 31:23 T.M.

_____
_____
_____
_____
_____
_____
_____
_____
_____
_____
_____
_____
_____
_____
_____
_____
_____
_____
_____
_____
_____
_____

"Blessed God! His love is the wonder of the world."
Psalm 31:22 T.M.

"Love God, all you saints; God takes care of all who stay close to him."
Psalm 31:23 T.M.

_____

_____

_____

_____

_____

_____

_____

_____

_____

_____

_____

_____

_____

_____

_____

_____

_____

_____

_____

_____

"Be brave. Be strong. Don't give up. Expect God to get here soon."
Psalm 31:24 T.M.

_____
_____
_____
_____
_____
_____
_____
_____
_____
_____
_____
_____
_____
_____
_____
_____
_____
_____
_____
_____
_____

"Count yourself lucky, how happy you must be___ you get a fresh start, your slate's wiped clean." Psalm 32:1 T.M.

_____

_____

_____

_____

_____

_____

_____

_____

_____

_____

_____

_____

_____

_____

_____

_____

_____

_____

_____

_____

"These things add up. Every one of us needs to pray; when all hell breaks loose and the dam bursts we'll be on high ground, untouched." Psalm 32.6 T.M.

"God's my island hideaway, keeps danger far from the shore, throws garlands of hosannas around my neck." Psalm 32:7 T.M.

_____

_____

_____

_____

_____

_____

_____

_____

_____

_____

_____

_____

_____

_____

_____

_____

_____

_____

_____

_____

_____

_____

_____

"For God's word is solid to the core; everything he makes
is sound inside and out." Psalm 33:4 T.M.

"Earth is drenched in God's affectionate satisfaction."
Psalm 33:5 T.M.

_____

_____

_____

_____

_____

_____

_____

_____

_____

_____

_____

_____

_____

_____

_____

_____

_____

_____

_____

_____

_____

_____

_____

"Watch this. God's eye is on those who respect him, the ones who are looking for his love." Psalm 33:18 T. M.

"He's ready to come to their rescue in bad times; in lean times
he keeps body and soul together." Psalm 33:19 T.M.

_____

_____

_____

_____

_____

_____

_____

_____

_____

_____

_____

_____

_____

_____

_____

_____

_____

_____

_____

_____

_____

_____

_____

"God met me more than half way, he freed me from my anxious fears."
Psalm 34:4 T.M.

_____
_____
_____
_____
_____
_____
_____
_____
_____
_____
_____
_____
_____
_____
_____
_____
_____
_____
_____
_____
_____
_____

"Look at him; give him your warmest smile.   Never hide your feelings from him." Psalm 34:5 T.M.

_____

_____

_____

_____

_____

_____

_____

_____

_____

_____

_____

_____

_____

_____

_____

_____

_____

_____

_____

_____

_____

_____

_____

"When I was desperate, I called out, and God got me out of a tight spot." Psalm 34:6 T.M.

"God's angel sets up a circle of protection around us while we pray."
Psalm 34:7 T.M.

_____
_____
_____
_____
_____
_____
_____
_____
_____
_____
_____
_____
_____
_____
_____
_____
_____
_____
_____
_____
_____
_____

*"Open your mouth and taste, open your eyes and see__how good God is.
Blessed are you who run to him." Psalm 34:8 T.M.*

"Worship God if you want the best; worship opens doors to all his goodness."
Psalm 34:9 T. M.

"Young lions on the prowl get hungry, but God-seekers are full of God."
Psalm 34:10 T.M.

"Is anyone crying for help? God is listening, ready to rescue you."
Psalm 34:17 T.M.

"If your heart is broken, you'll find God right there; if you're kicked in the gut, he'll help you catch your breath." Psalm 34:18 T.M.

"Disciples so often get into trouble; still, God is there every time."
Psalm 34:19 T.M.

_____

_____

_____

_____

_____

_____

_____

_____

_____

_____

_____

_____

_____

_____

_____

_____

_____

_____

_____

_____

_____

_____

"God pays free each slave's freedom, no one who runs to him loses out."
Psalm 34:22 T.M.

"But let me loose and free, celebrating God's great work,"
Psalm 25:9 T.M.

"You put the down-and-out on their feet and protect the unprotected from bullies!" Psalm 35:10 T.M.

"God is great __everything works together for good for his servant."
Psalm 35.28 T. M.

_____
_____
_____
_____
_____
_____
_____
_____
_____
_____
_____
_____
_____
_____
_____
_____
_____
_____
_____
_____
_____
_____

*"How exquisite your love, O God! How eager
we are to run under your wings." Psalm 36:7 T.M.*

"Keep company with God, get in on the best."
Psalm 37:4 T.M.

"Open up before God, keep nothing back; he'll do whatever needs to be done."
Psalm 37:5 T.M.

"He'll validate your life in the clear light of day and stamp you with approval at high noon." Psalm 37:6 T. M.

"Quiet down before God, be prayerful before him."
Psalm 37:7 T.M.

"God keeps track of the decent folk; what they do won't soon be forgotten."
Psalm 37:18 T. M.

_____
_____
_____
_____
_____
_____
_____
_____
_____
_____
_____
_____
_____
_____
_____
_____
_____
_____
_____
_____
_____

"In hard times they'll hold their heads high; when the shelves are bare, they'll be full." Psalm 37:19 T.M.

"Stalwart walks in step with God; his path blazed by God, he's happy. If he stumbles, he's not down for long; God has a grip on his hand." Psalm 37:24

_____
_____
_____
_____
_____
_____
_____
_____
_____
_____
_____
_____
_____
_____
_____
_____
_____
_____
_____
_____
_____

"Wait passionately for God, don't leave the path."
Psalm 37:34 T.M.

_____
_____
_____
_____
_____
_____
_____
_____
_____
_____
_____
_____
_____
_____
_____
_____
_____
_____
_____
_____
_____
_____
_____
_____

"He'll give you're your place in the sun while you watch the wicked lose it."
Psalm 37:34 T.M

_____

_____

_____

_____

_____

_____

_____

_____

_____

_____

_____

_____

_____

_____

_____

_____

_____

_____

_____

_____

_____

_____

"The spacious, free life is from God, it's also protected and safe."
Psalm 37:39 T.M.

"God-strengthened, we're delivered from evil__when we run to him he saves us." Psalm 37:40 T.M.

"He lifted me out of the ditch, pulled me from the deep mud."
Psalm 40:1 T.M.

"He stood me up on a solid rock to make sure I wouldn't slip."
Psalm 40.2 T.M

_____

_____

_____

_____

_____

_____

_____

_____

_____

_____

_____

_____

_____

_____

_____

_____

_____

_____

_____

_____

_____

_____

*"Embrace this God-life. Really embrace it,
and nothing will be too much for you.."
Mark 11:22 T.M.*

"This mountain, for instance: Just say, 'Go jump in the lake'___no shuffling or shilly-shallying___and it's as good as done." Mark 11:23 T.M

_____

_____

_____

_____

_____

_____

_____

_____

_____

_____

_____

_____

_____

_____

_____

_____

_____

_____

_____

_____

_____

"That's why I urge you to pray for absolutely everything, ranging from small to large." Mark 11:24 T.M.

_____
_____
_____
_____
_____
_____
_____
_____
_____
_____
_____
_____
_____
_____
_____
_____
_____
_____
_____
_____
_____
_____

*"I am the Good Shepherd. I know my own sheep
and my own sheep know me." John 10:14*

_____

_____

_____

_____

_____

_____

_____

_____

_____

_____

_____

_____

_____

_____

_____

_____

_____

_____

_____

_____

_____

"My sheep recognize my voice. I know them, and they follow me."
John 10:27 T.M.

"Let me give you a new command: Love one another. In the same way I love you, you love one another." John 13:34 T.M.

_____

_____

_____

_____

_____

_____

_____

_____

_____

_____

_____

_____

_____

_____

_____

_____

_____

_____

_____

"The Friend, the Holy Spirit whom the Father will send at my request, will make everything plain to you." John 14:25 T.M.

"But if you make yourselves at home with me and my words at home in you, you can be sure that whatever you ask will be listened to and acted upon." John 15:7 T.M

_____

_____

_____

_____

_____

_____

_____

_____

_____

_____

_____

_____

_____

_____

_____

_____

_____

_____

_____

_____

_____

"You're far happier giving than getting."
Acts 20.35 T.M.

"That's why we can be so sure that every detail in our lives of love for God is worked into something good." Romans 8:28 T. M.

_____

_____

_____

_____

_____

_____

_____

_____

_____

_____

_____

_____

_____

_____

_____

_____

_____

_____

_____

_____

_____

_____

"So, what do you think? With God on our side like this,
how can we lose?" Romans 8:31 T.M.

_____

_____

_____

_____

_____

_____

_____

_____

_____

_____

_____

_____

_____

_____

_____

_____

_____

_____

_____

_____

_____

_____

*"Yet in all things we are more than conquerors,
through him who loved us." Romans 8:37 N.K.J.V.*

_____
_____
_____
_____
_____
_____
_____
_____
_____
_____
_____
_____
_____
_____
_____
_____
_____
_____
_____

"For I am persuaded that neither death nor life, nor angels nor principalities, nor powers, nor things present, nor things to come... shall be able to separate from the love of God."

Romans 8:37 N.K.J.V.

"So then faith comes by hearing, and hearing by the word of God."
Romans 10.17 N. K. J. V.

"Now abides faith, hope, love, these three;
but the greatest of these is love." 1 Corinthians 13:13 N.K.J.V.

_____
_____
_____
_____
_____
_____
_____
_____
_____
_____
_____
_____
_____
_____
_____
_____
_____
_____
_____
_____
_____

"He who sows sparingly, will also reap sparingly, and he who sows bountifully will also reap bountifully." 2 Corinthians 9:6 N.K.J.V.

_____

_____

_____

_____

_____

_____

_____

_____

_____

_____

_____

_____

_____

_____

_____

_____

_____

_____

_____

_____

_____

"So let each one give as he purposes in his heart, not grudgingly or of necessity, for God loves a cheerful giver." 2 Corinthians 9:7 N. K. J. V.

_____

_____

_____

_____

_____

_____

_____

_____

_____

_____

_____

_____

_____

_____

_____

_____

_____

_____

_____

_____

_____

_____

_____

"And God is able to make all grace abound towards you."
2 Corinthians 9:8 N.K.J.V.

_____

_____

_____

_____

_____

_____

_____

_____

_____

_____

_____

_____

_____

_____

_____

_____

_____

_____

_____

_____

"that you having all sufficiency in all things, may have an abundance for every good work." 2 Corinthians 9:8 N.K.J.V.

"But God who is rich in mercy, because of his great love with which he loved us."
Ephesians 2:4 N. K. J. V.

_____
_____
_____
_____
_____
_____
_____
_____
_____
_____
_____
_____
_____
_____
_____
_____
_____
_____
_____
_____
_____
_____

"Now to him who is able to do exceedingly abundantly above all we ask or think, according to the power that works in us." Ephesians 3:20 N.K.J.V.

"Be anxious for nothing, but in everything by prayer and supplication with
thanksgiving let your requests be made known to God."
Philippians 4:6 N.K.J.V.

"and the peace of God which surpasses all understanding will guard your hearts and minds through Christ Jesus." Philippians 4:6 N.K.J.V.

"Whatever things are true, whatever things are noble, whatever things are just... meditate on these things." Philippians 4:8 N.K.J.V.

*"But above all these things put on love,
which is the bond of perfection." Colossians 3:14 N. K. J. V.*

"And let the peace of God rule in your hearts, to which also you were called in one body, and be thankful." Colossians 3:14 N. K. J. V.

"For God has not given us a spirit of fear, but of power and of love and of a sound mind." 2 Timothy 1:7 N.K.J.V.

"Let us hold fast the confession of our hope without wavering, for he who promised is faithful." Hebrews 10:23 N.K.J.V.

"But you O Lord, are a shield around me."
Psalm 3:3 N.L.T.

"I cried out to the Lord and he answered me from his holy mountain."
Psalm 3:4 N.L.T.

_____

_____

_____

_____

_____

_____

_____

_____

_____

_____

_____

_____

_____

_____

_____

_____

_____

_____

_____

*"I lay down and slept. I woke up in safety, for the Lord
was watching over me." Psalm 3:5 N.L.T.*

_____
_____
_____
_____
_____
_____
_____
_____
_____
_____
_____
_____
_____
_____
_____
_____
_____
_____
_____
_____
_____
_____

"Victory comes from you, O Lord.
May your blessings rest on your people." Psalm 3:8 N.L.T.

"You can be sure of this: The Lord has set apart the Godly for himself."
Psalm 4:3 N.L.T.

"You have given me greater joy than those who have abundant harvests of grain and wine."
Psalm 4:7 N.L.T.

_____

_____

_____

_____

_____

_____

_____

_____

_____

_____

_____

_____

_____

_____

_____

_____

_____

_____

_____

_____

"I will lie down in peace and sleep, for you alone, O Lord will keep me safe.
Psalm 4:8 N.L.T.

"But let all who take refuge in you rejoice."
Psalm 5:11 N.L.T.

_____

_____

_____

_____

_____

_____

_____

_____

_____

_____

_____

_____

_____

_____

_____

_____

_____

_____

_____

_____

_____

"God is my shield, saving those whose hearts are true and right."
Psalm 7:10 N.L.T.

"When I look at the night sky and see the work of your fingers, the moon and the stars that you have set in place, what mortals that you should think of us?"
Psalm 8:3 N.L.T

_____

_____

_____

_____

_____

_____

_____

_____

_____

_____

_____

_____

_____

_____

_____

_____

_____

_____

_____

_____

_____

_____

_____

"Lord, you know the hopes of the helpless. Surely you will listen to their cries and bring them comfort." Psalm 10:17 N.L.T.

"I will sing to the Lord because he has been so good to me."
Psalm 13:6 N.L.T.

_____

_____

_____

_____

_____

_____

_____

_____

_____

_____

_____

_____

_____

_____

_____

_____

_____

_____

_____

"Keep me safe O God, for I have come to you for refuge."
Psalm 16:1 N.L.T.

"Lord you alone are my inheritance, my cup of blessing. You guard all that is mine."
Psalm 16:5 N.L.T.

"The land you have given me is a pleasant land. What a wonderful inheritance!"
Psalm 16:5 N.L.T.

"I will bless the Lord who guides me; even at night my heart instructs me."
Psalm 16:7 N.L.T.

"You will show me the way of life, granting me the joy of your presence, and the pleasures of living with you forever." Psalm 17:17 N.L.T.

"I love you, Lord; you are my strength. The Lord is my rock, my fortress and my savior." Psalm 18:2 N.L.T.

_____

_____

_____

_____

_____

_____

_____

_____

_____

_____

_____

_____

_____

_____

_____

_____

_____

_____

_____

"My God is my rock in whom I will find protection."
Psalm 18:2 N.L.T.

"The heavens tell of the Glory of God."
Psalm 19:1 N.L.T.

_____

_____

_____

_____

_____

_____

_____

_____

_____

_____

_____

_____

_____

_____

_____

_____

_____

_____

_____

_____

"The skies display his marvelous craftsmanship."
Psalm 19:1 N.L.T.

"Day after day they continue to speak;
night after night they make him known." Psalm 19:1 N.L.T.

"They speak without a sound or a word; their voices are silent in the skies; yet their message has gone out to all the earth and their words to all the world." Psalm 19:1 N.L.T.

"Lord, you brought light to my life; my God,
you light up my darkness."
Psalm 18:28 N.L.T.

"As for God, his way is perfect.
All the Lord's promises prove true."
Psalm 18:30 N.L.T.

"God arms me with strength; he has made my way safe."
Psalm 18:32 N.L.T.

"You have given me the shield of your salvation."
Psalm 18:35 N.L.T.

"Your right hand supports me;
your gentleness has made me great." Psalm 18:35 N.L.T.

_____

_____

_____

_____

_____

_____

_____

_____

_____

_____

_____

_____

_____

_____

_____

_____

_____

_____

_____

_____

"You have made a wide path for my feet
to keep them from slipping." Psalm 18:35 N.L.T.

_____

_____

_____

_____

_____

_____

_____

_____

_____

_____

_____

_____

_____

_____

_____

_____

_____

_____

_____

_____

"You have armed me with strength for the battle;
you have subdued my enemies under my feet."
Psalm 18:39 N.L.T.

"May he send you help from his sanctuary."
Psalm 20:2 N.L.T.

"May he grant your heart's desire and fulfill all your plans." Psalm 20:4 N.L.T.

_____

_____

_____

_____

_____

_____

_____

_____

_____

_____

_____

_____

_____

_____

_____

_____

_____

_____

_____

_____

_____

"You welcomed him back with success and prosperity."
Psalm 21:3 N.L.T.

"The Lord is my shepherd; I have everything I need."
Psalm 23:1 N.L.T.

"He lets me rest in green meadows;
he leads me beside peaceful streams." Psalm 23:2 N.L.T.

"He renews my strength."
Psalm 23:3 N.L.T.

_____

_____

_____

_____

_____

_____

_____

_____

_____

_____

_____

_____

_____

_____

_____

_____

_____

_____

_____

_____

_____

"he guides me along right paths,
bringing honor to his name." Psalm 23:3 N.L.T.

"If I could speak all the languages of earth, and of angels, but didn't love others, I would be a noisy gong or clanging cymbal." 1 Corinthians 13:1 N.L.T.

"and if I had such faith that I could move mountains, but didn't love others, I would be nothing." 1 Corinthians 13:2 N.L.T.

"Love is patient and kind. Love is not jealous or boastful or proud or rude." 1 Corinthians 13:4 N.L.T.

"Love does not demand its own way. It is not irritable, \and keeps no record of being wronged." 1 Corinthians 13:5 N.L.T.

*"Love does not rejoice about injustice but rejoices
whenever the truth wins out."* 1 Corinthians 13:5 N.L.T.

"*Love never gives up, never loses faith, is always hopeful, and endures through every circumstance.*" 1 Corinthians 13:6 N.L.T.

*"But when full understanding comes,
these partial things will become useless."* 1 Corinthians 13:10 N.L.T.

"When I was a child, I spoke and thought and reasoned as a child. But when I grew up I put away childish things." 1 Corinthians 13:11 N.L.T.

*"Now we see things imperfectly as in a cloudy mirror,
but then we will see everything with perfect clarity."* 1 Corinthians 13:12 N.L.T.

_____

_____

_____

_____

_____

_____

_____

_____

_____

_____

_____

_____

_____

_____

_____

_____

_____

_____

_____

_____

_____

_____

*These things will last forever, faith, hope, and love,
and the greatest of these is love." 1 Corin"thians 13:13 N.L.T.*

"I always thank my God for you and for the gracious gifts he has given you." 1 Corinthians 1:4 N.L.T.

_____

_____

_____

_____

_____

_____

_____

_____

_____

_____

_____

_____

_____

_____

_____

_____

_____

_____

_____

_____

"For his Spirit searches out everything and shows us God's deep secrets." 1 Corinthians 2:10 N.L.T.

_____
_____
_____
_____
_____
_____
_____
_____
_____
_____
_____
_____
_____
_____
_____
_____
_____
_____
_____
_____

"and we received God's Spirit so we can know the wonderful things God has freely given us." 1 Corinthians 2:12 N.L.T.

"For the kingdom of God is not just a lot of talk;
it is living by God's power." 1 Corinthians 4:20 N.L.T.

*"All of you together are Christ's body,
and each of you is a part of it."* Corinthians 12:27 N.L.T.

_____

_____

_____

_____

_____

_____

_____

_____

_____

_____

_____

_____

_____

_____

_____

_____

_____

_____

_____

_____

*"He comforts us in all our troubles
so we can comfort others." 2 Corinthians 1:4 N.L.T.*

"For the Lord is the Spirit and wherever
the Spirit of the Lord is there is freedom." 2 Corinthians 3:17 N.L.T.

"We are pressed on every side by trouble, but we are not crushed. We are perplexed, but not driven to despair." 2 Corinthians 4:8 N.L.T.

_____

_____

_____

_____

_____

_____

_____

_____

_____

_____

_____

_____

_____

_____

_____

_____

_____

_____

_____

_____

"For our present troubles are small and won't last very long. Yet they produce for us a glory that vastly outweighs them and will last forever."
2 Corinthians 4:17 N.L.T.

"For the things we now see will soon be gone, but the things we cannot see will last forever." 2 Corinthians 4:18 N.L.T.

"For we live by believing and not by seeing."
2 Corinthians 5:7 N.L.T.

"I will live in them and walk among them.
I will be their God, and they will be my people." 2 Corinthians 6:16b N.L.T.

"and I will be your Father, and you will be my sons and daughters, says the Lord almighty." 2 Corinthians 6:18 N.L.T.

_____
_____
_____
_____
_____
_____
_____
_____
_____
_____
_____
_____
_____
_____
_____
_____
_____
_____
_____
_____
_____

*"But God, who encourages those
who are discouraged, encouraged us."* 2 Corinthians 7.6 N.L.T.

"Remember the farmer who plants only a few seeds will get a small crop. But the one who plants generously will get a generous crop." 2 Corinthians 9:6 N.L.T.

"And God will generously provide all you need."
2 Corinthians 9:8 N.L.T.

"Then you will always have everything you need and plenty left over to share with others." 2 Corinthians 9:8 N.L.T.

"For God is the one who gives seed
to the farmer and then bread to eat." 2 Corinthians 9:10 N.L.T.

"In the same way, he will give you many opportunities to do good, and he will produce a great harvest of generosity in you." 2 Corinthians 9:10 N.L.T.

"Take hold of my instructions, and don't let them go. Guard them for they are the keys of life." Proverbs 4:13 N.L.T.

"The way of the righteous is like the first gleam of dawn which shines ever brighter until the full light of day." Proverbs 4:18 N.L.T.

"Guard your heart above all else,
for it determines the course of your life." Proverbs 4:23 N.L.T.

"Look straight ahead, and fix your eyes on what lies before you." Proverbs 4:25 N.L.T.

_____

_____

_____

_____

_____

_____

_____

_____

_____

_____

_____

_____

_____

_____

_____

_____

_____

_____

_____

_____

"Mark out a straight path for your feet, stay on the safe path. Don't get sidetracked; keep your feet from following evil." Proverbs 4:25, 26 N.L.T.

"Keep my words always in your heart."
Proverbs 6:21 N.L.T.

_____

_____

_____

_____

_____

_____

_____

_____

_____

_____

_____

_____

_____

_____

_____

_____

_____

_____

_____

_____

_____

_____

*"Choose my instruction rather than silver
and knowledge rather than pure gold." Proverbs 8:10 N.L.T.*

_____
_____
_____
_____
_____
_____
_____
_____
_____
_____
_____
_____
_____
_____
_____
_____
_____
_____
_____
_____
_____
_____

*"For wisdom is far more valuable than rubies.
Nothing you desire can compare with it." Proverbs 8:10 N.L.T.*

"Common sense and success belong to me.
Insight and strength are mine." Proverbs 8:14 N.L.T.

"I love all those who love me.
Those who search will surely find me." Proverbs 8:17 N.L.T.

*"My gifts are better than gold, even the purest gold,
my wages are better than sterling silver." Proverbs 8:19 N.L.T.*

"And so, my children listen to me.
For all who follow my ways are joyful." Proverbs 8:32 N.L.T.

_____

_____

_____

_____

_____

_____

_____

_____

_____

_____

_____

_____

_____

_____

_____

_____

_____

_____

"Joyful are those who listen to me, watching for me daily at my gates, waiting for me outside my home!" Proverbs 8:34 N.L.T.

"For whoever finds me finds life
and receives favor from the Lord." Proverbs 8:35 N.L.T.

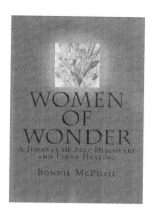

Product Description
<u>Women of Wonder</u> is an eight-week program for women. It can be completed privately or in a group, and includes an instructor's guide. Through the program, you will discover biblical perspectives about your own personality, talents and ministry gifts, as well as lessons about the gifts of the Spirit. It also includes guidelines for women's health and fitness. In addition, W.O.W. includes a beautiful inner healing devotional, and inspirational "Life Songs." This is a must for women of all ages, and is truly life-changing!

Editorial Reviews

Product Description

Friends and Gems is a four week course covering a different topic for each week, the lessons can be done separately or with a group of women. The lessons are from a biblical perspective and include: God Has a Miracle for You Discovering Your Own Personality Health and Wellness Tips for Women How to Listen to the Voice of the Father Each lesson comes with an instructor's guide. There will also be classroom instruction with step by step black and white photos for the following workshops: Fundamentals of Soap Making Making a Container Candle Aroma Bead Sachets The Art of Making Hand Crafted Note Cards You can spend time with your gal pals learning wonderful biblical truths and how to make beautiful hand crafted items.

Inspirational Blank Journals

Each of these beautiful journals contain 200 blank pages with scriptures and either a poem, song or short story.

Journaling accompanied with the Word of God is a powerful tool to obtain your dreams and receive wisdom and insight.

NEW CHAPTER BOOK FOR KIDS!

While trying to find his way home from being lost in the woods, Danny discovers a secret that will take him on an adventure requiring him to risk his life to save his father.

Betrayed for the Alaskan Secret is a middle reader chapter book that underscores the importance of prayer and biblical concepts in resolving real life situations.

Other Books by Bonnie McPhail available on
TheFathersMarket.com
Contact the author at: angelcare6@yahoo.com

10818505R00124

Made in the USA
Charleston, SC
07 January 2012